Scaly
Creatures

By Clint Twist

WATERBIRD BOOKS
Columbus, Ohio

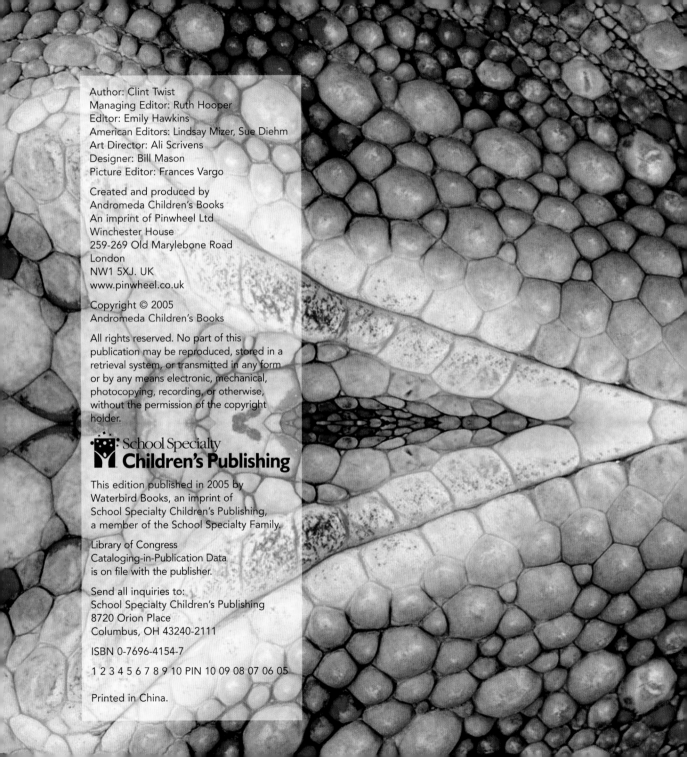

Author: Clint Twist
Managing Editor: Ruth Hooper
Editor: Emily Hawkins
American Editors: Lindsay Mizer, Sue Diehm
Art Director: Ali Scrivens
Designer: Bill Mason
Picture Editor: Frances Vargo

Created and produced by
Andromeda Children's Books
An imprint of Pinwheel Ltd
Winchester House
259-269 Old Marylebone Road
London
NW1 5XJ. UK
www.pinwheel.co.uk

School Specialty
Children's Publishing

This edition published in 2005 by
Waterbird Books, an imprint of
School Specialty Children's Publishing,
a member of the School Specialty Family.

Library of Congress
Cataloging-in-Publication Data
is on file with the publisher.

Send all inquiries to:
School Specialty Children's Publishing
8720 Orion Place
Columbus, OH 43240-2111

ISBN 0-7696-4154-7

1 2 3 4 5 6 7 8 9 10 PIN 10 09 08 07 06 05

Printed in China.

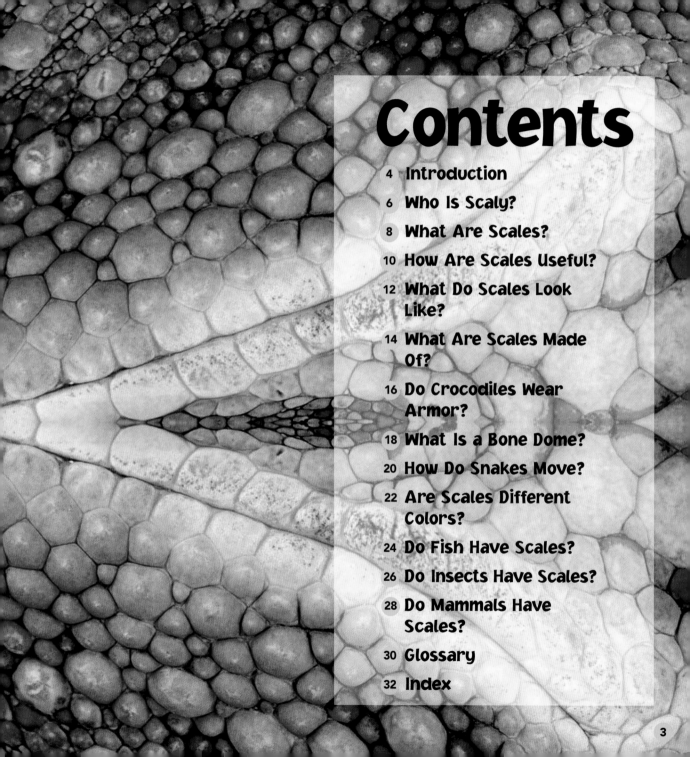

Contents

Introduction

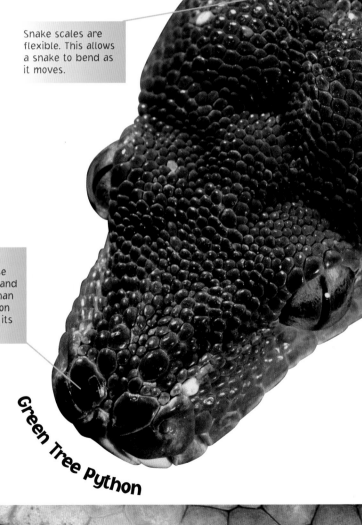

Many different animals in the world have scales. These scales cover their skins. Scales help protect and identify animals. Sometimes, scales help animals move.

Snake scales are flexible. This allows a snake to bend as it moves.

DID YOU KNOW?

Sometimes, scaly animals look as if they are wet. This is really just light reflecting off their shiny scales.

Scales on a snake's nose are larger and stronger than the scales on the rest of its body.

Green Tree Python

As a snake grows, it sheds its outer layer of scales and grows a new one.

Snake Scales

Snakes have different types of scales on their bodies. Some scales are used for protection. Others are used for movement.

Crocodile Scales

Crocodile Scales

Crocodile scales look very different from snake or lizard scales. Crocodile scales are much thicker and tougher. They also have a more unusual shape.

Emerald Tree Skink

Smooth and Shiny

A layer of small, thin scales gives many lizards, such as this emerald tree skink, a very smooth, shiny appearance.

FASCINATING SCALY FACT

Skinks are a type of lizard. Some skinks do not have legs. To move, they wriggle through loose sand or soil.

Who Is Scaly?

Gila Monster

Reptiles are scaly. Reptiles are lizards, snakes, crocodiles, alligators, and turtles. Most fish have scales. Some mammals also have scales.

Smooth Scales

Most lizards, like this Gila monster, are covered with small scales. From a distance, these reptiles look as if they have smooth skin. The scales can only be seen up close.

Alligator Snapping Turtle

Hard Shell Scales

A turtle is a reptile that has small scales on its head and legs. A shell made of larger scales protects its body.

DID YOU KNOW?

A number of baby reptiles hatch from eggs. When they hatch, they are completely covered with scales.

A lizard uses its tongue to taste and smell its surroundings.

Salmon

The scales of the Gila monster are raised and round. They look like tiny beads.

Glittering Scales

Fish, like these salmon, often seem to glitter. This is caused by light reflecting off their scales.

FASCINATING SCALY FACT

Lizards and snakes use their tongues to collect samples of tastes and scents. They store them in a special sense organ in the roof of their mouths.

What Are Scales?

Scales are plates of hard material. Scales form in or on the skin of an animal. An outer layer of scales covers most reptiles and fish.

Rattlesnake

Rattle Scales

A rattlesnake sheds its outer layer of skin like other snakes. But rattlesnakes always keep one old tail scale. This one scale builds up on the tip of the tail to form the snake's special rattle.

The small scales on an iguana's legs overlap. They form a flexible outer coat.

Spiny Scales

An iguana has scales along its back that are shaped like sharp spines. They give this reptile a fearsome appearance.

Green Iguana

DID YOU KNOW?

Some geckos make good pets. These harmless lizards catch flies and other insect pests.

Gecko Foot

The large scales on an iguana's head fit close together. Its head does not need the flexibility of small, overlapping scales.

Geckos

The gecko is a type of lizard. Most geckos' feet are covered with tiny, overlapping scales. The scales spread out at the tips of the toes. This allows the geckos to grip smooth surfaces.

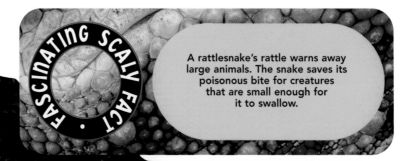

FASCINATING SCALY FACT

A rattlesnake's rattle warns away large animals. The snake saves its poisonous bite for creatures that are small enough for it to swallow.

How Are Scales Useful?

Skin is usually very soft and easily injured. Scales provide a layer of protection against attacks. Scales also provide camouflage, support, and identification.

Large scales cover the snake's head.

Scales for Camouflage

Chameleon Scales

Some scales form patterns on an animal's skin. They help the animal blend in with its surroundings. Attackers usually cannot see the animal. This is called *camouflage*.

Scales for Support

Fish Scales

Most fish scales are thin and clear. They protect the fish and help to support the shape of its body.

Scales for Identification

Snake Scales

Each scale on a snake can be a different color. Many snakes have detailed patterns that make them easy to identify.

Milk Snake

FASCINATING SCALY FACTS •

Thorny Devil

The fierce-looking thorny devil is actually a harmless reptile. Some of its scales are spiky for protection.

Some animals have colors and patterns that look like other animals. These animals are called *mimics*.

This snake has a distinctive pattern of colored stripes.

These small scales fit closely together. They help the snake move forward and turn around.

Scales of Confusion

This harmless milk snake has colorful stripes that look like the stripes of another very dangerous snake. This makes attackers stay away from it.

What Do Scales Look Like?

Scales come in all different shapes, colors, and sizes. Sometimes, they are smooth, shiny, and fit together like the tiles on a floor. Sometimes, they are shaped like shields and overlap each other.

Crocodile Skink

Spiny Skinks

The crocodile skink has scales that end in raised spines.

The ridge in the center of each scale is called the *keel*.

Shield-Shaped Scales

This is a photograph of snake scales up close. The scales are shaped like shields and overlap each other. Each scale is gently curved so that it will fit around the snake's round body.

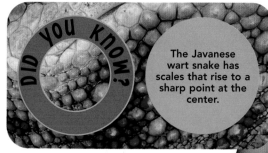

DID YOU KNOW?

The Javanese wart snake has scales that rise to a sharp point at the center.

Scaly or Hairy?

The hairy bush viper gets its name from its scales. Each scale comes to a fine point. It makes the snake look "hairy."

The scales around the eyes do not have points.

FASCINATING SCALY FACT •

The number of rows of scales on a snake's body varies from less than 10 to more than 100.

Hairy Bush Viper

The scales always point in the direction of the viper's tail.

What Are Scales Made Of?

Scales are made of very hard materials. Fish, crocodile, and turtle scales are made of a bony substance. Other reptiles have scales that are of the same material as horns and fingernails.

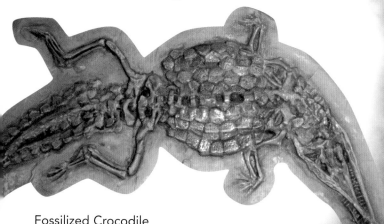

Fossilized Crocodile

Scutes and Bones

Bony scales, called *scutes*, protect the bodies of crocodiles and alligators. A large number of scutes can be seen among the fossilized bones of this prehistoric crocodile.

The growth rings on a fish's scales tell its age.

Rainbow Boa

Feathery Scales

The scales of snakes and lizards grow from the upper layer of skin, like feathers and hairs. They are also made from a similar material.

Growth Rings

Unlike the scales of snakes and lizards, fish scales grow as the fish increases in size.

Fish scales have both smooth and rough edges.

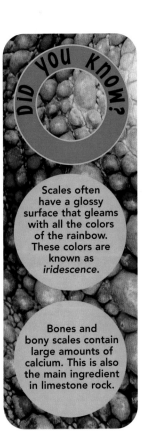

DID YOU KNOW?

Scales often have a glossy surface that gleams with all the colors of the rainbow. These colors are known as *iridescence*.

Bones and bony scales contain large amounts of calcium. This is also the main ingredient in limestone rock.

Do Crocodiles Wear Armor?

DID YOU KNOW?

Some crocodiles and alligators are in danger of extinction. People want their skins to make belts, bags, and shoes.

Crocodiles and alligators have thick, tough skins. Their skins are made even tougher by bony scutes. These scutes protect the animal, just like a coat of armor.

Tough on Top

Alligators and crocodiles are closely related. Their armor plating follows the same pattern, giving the animals a rough and rugged appearance.

The scales on the underside of this alligator are smaller and less bony than those on its back.

Saltwater Crocodiles

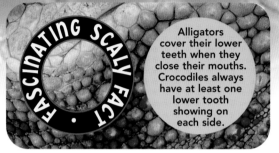

FASCINATING SCALY FACT ·

Alligators cover their lower teeth when they close their mouths. Crocodiles always have at least one lower tooth showing on each side.

Scaly Monsters

Saltwater crocodiles are the largest and fiercest reptiles in the world. The bony scutes on their backs are almost as big as dinner plates.

Deadly Log

A crocodile spends many hours half-submerged in water. From a distance, its rough scales make it look like an innocent log!

American alligator

The gharial crocodile's long jaws and sharp teeth help it firmly grip slippery fish.

Gharial Crocodile

What Is a Bone Dome?

The inside of the carapace is bony. The outer layer is made of the same substance as snake and lizard scales.

Giant Tortoi[se]

Turtles are protected by a dome-shaped shell. This dome is called a *carapace*. The carapace is a part of the turtle's skeleton. It is usually made from large, bony scutes.

Green Turtle

Sea Turtles

Sea turtles are becoming rare. They are hunted for their meat and their carapaces, which are used for decoration.

The underside of the carapace is called the *plastron*.

Each of the individual scutes on the carapace is slightly dome-shaped.

Flatter Figure

In some cases, the scutes of the carapace are not joined tightly together. Instead, they are loosely connected. This makes the carapace flexible. The pancake tortoise is able to flatten itself so it can crawl beneath rocks.

Pancake Tortoise

FASCINATING SCALY FACT ·

The largest turtle is the elephant tortoise from the Galapagos Islands. One grew to more than 4¼ feet in length.

Armored Giants

Turtles do not shed their skins. They just keep on growing. The giant tortoise is the biggest of all turtles. It grows so big because it lives for more than 100 years!

If it senses danger, a turtle can pull its head and legs inside its shell.

How Do Snakes Move?

Snakes use special scales on the underside of their bodies to move around. The outer edges of these scales dig into the ground. This allows them to push themselves forward.

Cobra

Belly Scales

Each scale on a cobra's belly reaches from one side of the snake's body to the other.

DID YOU KNOW?

Some small, burrowing snakes do not have special belly scales. They have the same small scales all over their bodies.

Tree Snake

Special scales run the entire length of a tree snake's belly, allowing it to grip the tree.

Desert Sands

Most snakes move head first, but this side-winding snake uses a different method. It flings its body sideways in a series of twisting, *S*-shaped loops.

Tree Climbers

Many snakes are excellent tree climbers. They push themselves up tree trunks as easily as they move along the ground. Their flexible bodies allow them to change direction easily when climbing through branches.

A flexible covering of scales allows the snake to twist and turn as it climbs.

Peringuey's Viper

FASCINATING SCALY FACT

Some snakes spend most of their time in the water. These snakes have little use for walking scales. They swim by moving their bodies from side to side.

Are Scales Different Colors?

Scales come in all different colors. Lizards from tropical rainforests are among the most brightly colored animals on earth. Most other lizards have less colorful scales because camouflage is important. Sometimes, brightly colored scales carry coded messages.

Warning Sign

The Gila monster's pink scales are a warning sign to attackers. This lizard has a poisonous bite.

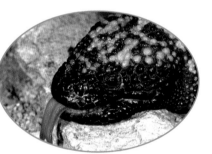

Gila Monster

FASCINATING SCALY FACTS •

The Ibiza wall lizard is bright blue with black spots.

The color of a male iguana becomes brighter during its breeding period.

Chameleons are well adapted for life in the trees. They can hold on to branches with all four feet and their long, curling tails.

Stripes of color on this chameleon help disguise it from attackers.

Parson's Chameleon

Panther Chameleon

Changing Colors

Chameleons have the amazing ability to change colors. They can control the size of special color cells in their skin. Their color helps them blend in with their surroundings.

Chameleon

Feeling Blue

Chameleons change colors according to their moods. Their brightest colors are used to frighten away attackers or to attract a mate.

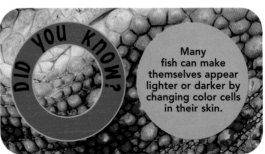

DID YOU KNOW?

Many fish can make themselves appear lighter or darker by changing color cells in their skin.

Do Fish Have Scales?

Most fish are covered in thin, round scales. A few fish, such as eels and catfish, have no scales at all.

Unusual Scales

Some fish, like this gar, have smaller and thicker scales than most fish. Their scales are usually diamond-shaped.

Overlapping scales give the carp's body flexibility for swimming.

The mirror carp's fins and tail do not have scales. They are stiffened by thin, bony rods.

Mirror Carp

Gar

Sharks

Sharks are fish that do not have an outer coating of thin scales. Instead, they have thousands of small, hard scales embedded in their skin.

Tiger Shark

Hard scales protect the skin against diseases.

Scaly Protection

An outer covering of scales protects most fish. These scales are colorless and clear, allowing the skin color to show through.

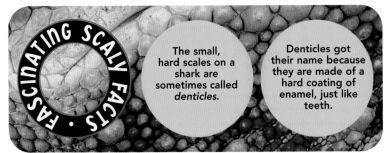

FASCINATING SCALY FACTS

The small, hard scales on a shark are sometimes called *denticles*.

Denticles got their name because they are made of a hard coating of enamel, just like teeth.

Do Insects Have Scales?

Butterflies and moths are the only insects that have scales. Their scales are very different from the scales found on reptiles or fish.

Unlike other insects that have hard outer coverings, a butterfly's body is covered with long, thin, hair-like scales.

Small Scales

Tiny, overlapping scales cover the wings of moths and butterflies. These scales are so small that they can be seen only through a microscope.

Light reflects off the surface of these wing scales, producing bright, rainbow colors.

Colorful Scales

There are millions of scales in many shades of color covering the wings of this morpho butterfly.

Pine Hawk Moth

Morpho Butterfly

FASCINATING SCALY FACT

Butterflies have taste sensors on their feet. They taste their food by standing on it!

Camouflage Moths

The scales on the wings of this moth make a pattern that matches the tree branch. This makes it very hard for attackers to see the moth.

Do Mammals Have Scales?

Some mammals do not have fur or hair covering their bodies. Instead, they have scales. Armadillos and pangolins use their scales for protection.

Hairs and Scales

Like almost all other mammals, the hairy armadillo has hair growing from its skin. However, like other armadillos, its body is also covered by bands of scales. The overlapping bands allow these armadillos to roll up into protective balls.

Hairy Armadillo

Armored Armadillo

The giant armadillo is the largest type of armadillo. It can grow to more than 3¼ feet, or the size of a large dog, in length. This is too big to roll into a protective ball. Instead, this armored giant lowers itself to the ground. The scales across its back protect its body.

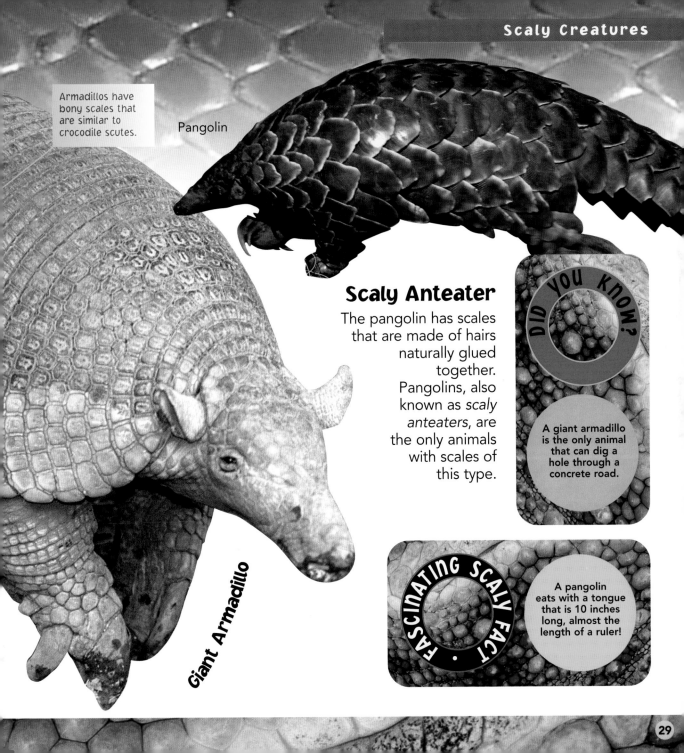

Armadillos have bony scales that are similar to crocodile scutes.

Pangolin

Scaly Anteater

The pangolin has scales that are made of hairs naturally glued together. Pangolins, also known as *scaly anteaters*, are the only animals with scales of this type.

Giant Armadillo

DID YOU KNOW?

A giant armadillo is the only animal that can dig a hole through a concrete road.

FASCINATING SCALY FACT

A pangolin eats with a tongue that is 10 inches long, almost the length of a ruler!

Glossary

Camouflage

Coloration or patterns that help an animal blend in with its surroundings. This makes it difficult for attackers to see the animal.

Carapace

The dome-shaped shell that protects turtles.

Denticles

The small, hard scales found in the skin of sharks.

Fossilized

Describes the remains of living things that have been preserved in the ground for millions of years.

Hair

Narrow fibers that grow from the skin of mammals and a few other animals.

Insect

A small animal with an exoskeleton instead of an internal skeleton and six jointed legs. Many insects have wings.

Iridescence

Rainbow colors that are created when light reflects off of glossy surfaces.

Keel

The ridge down the center of a scale.

Mammal

An animal with an internal skeleton arranged around a backbone. It breathes air through lungs and feeds its young on milk. The skin of mammals is usually protected by hair.

Mimic

An animal that has similar colors or patterns to another animal.

Reptile

An animal with scaly skin and an internal skeleton arranged around a backbone. It breathes air through its lungs. Reptiles are lizards, snakes, crocodiles, alligators, and turtles.

Scale

A small, hard structure that covers the skin of some animals.

Scute

A bony, larger than average scale, which protects the bodies of alligators, crocodiles, turtles, and tortoises.

Skeleton

A structure that provides support for an animal's body.

Skin

The soft, stretchy material that covers the bodies of animals that have an internal skeleton arranged around a backbone. Animal skin is usually protected by fur, feathers, scales, or slime.

Picture Credits

Index